SUPER
SANDCASTLE
Super Simple Cooking

Super Simple
Breakfasts

Easy No-Bake Recipes for Kids

Nancy Tuminelly

Consulting Editor, Diane Craig, M.A./Reading Specialist

ABDO
Publishing Company

Published by ABDO Publishing Company, 8000 West 78th Street, Edina, Minnesota 55439. Copyright © 2011 by Abdo Consulting Group, Inc. International copyrights reserved in all countries. No part of this book may be reproduced in any form without written permission from the publisher. Super SandCastle™ is a trademark and logo of ABDO Publishing Company.

Printed in the United States of America, North Mankato, Minnesota
052010
092010

 PRINTED ON RECYCLED PAPER

Editor: Katherine Hengel
Content Developer: Nancy Tuminelly
Cover and Interior Design and Production: Colleen Dolphin, Mighty Media
Photo Credits: Colleen Dolphin, iStockphoto (Tammy Bryngelson, Jami Garrison, Dawna Stafford), Shutterstock
Food Production: Colleen Dolphin, Katherine Hengel

The following manufacturers/names appearing in this book are trademarks:
Target® Aluminum Foil, Target® Plastic Wrap, Pyrex® Measuring Cup

Library of Congress Cataloging-in-Publication Data
Tuminelly, Nancy, 1952-
   Super simple breakfasts : easy no-bake recipes for kids / Nancy Tuminelly.
      p. cm. -- (Super simple cooking)
   ISBN 978-1-61613-383-2
   1. Breakfasts--Juvenile literature. 2. Quick and easy cookery--Juvenile literature. I. Title.
   TX733.T95 2011
   641.5'2--dc22
                                    2009053114

Super SandCastle™ books are created by a team of professional educators, reading specialists, and content developers around five essential components—phonemic awareness, phonics, vocabulary, text comprehension, and fluency—to assist young readers as they develop reading skills and strategies and increase their general knowledge. All books are written, reviewed, and leveled for guided reading, early reading intervention, and Accelerated Reader® programs for use in shared, guided, and independent reading and writing activities to support a balanced approach to literacy instruction.

Note to Adult Helpers

Helping kids learn how to cook is fun! It is a great way for them to practice math and science. Cooking teaches kids about responsibility and boosts their confidence. Plus, they learn how to help out in the kitchen! The recipes in this book require very little adult assistance. But make sure there is always an adult around when kids are in the kitchen. Expect kids to make a mess, but also expect them to clean up after themselves. Most importantly, make the experience pleasurable by sharing and enjoying the food kids make.

Symbols

 knife
Always ask an adult to help you cut with knives.

 microwave
Be careful with hot food! Learn more on page 5.

 nuts
Some people can get very sick if they eat nuts.

Contents

Let's Cook! 3

Cooking Basics..4

Measuring Tips..6

Cooking Terms 8

Tools 10

Ingredients 12

Breakfast in a Cone..............................14

Peanutty Banana Split 16

Waffle Sandwich...................................18

Rise 'n' Shine Rollup.............................20

Shake-Shake Shakes............................22

Ham & Cheese Bagel 24

Buenos Días Burrito 26

Sunny O's 28

Awesome Applesauce...........................30

Glossary..32

Let's Cook!

The recipes in this book are simple! You don't even need an oven or stove! Cooking teaches you about food, measuring, and following directions. It's fun to make good food! Enjoy your tasty creations with family and friends!

Bon appétit!

3

Cooking Basics

Before You Start...

- Get permission from an adult.
- Wash your hands.
- Read the recipe at least once.
- Set out all the ingredients, tools, and equipment you will need.
- Keep a towel close by for cleaning up spills.

When You're Done...

- Cover food with plastic wrap or **aluminum** foil. Use containers with tops when you can.
- Put all the ingredients and tools back where you found them.
- Wash all the dishes and **utensils**.
- Clean up your work space.

THINK SAFETY!

- Ask an adult to help you cut things. Use a cutting board.
- Clean up spills to prevent accidents.
- Keep tools and **utensils** away from the edge of the table or countertop.
- Keep potholders or oven mitts close to the microwave.
- Use a **sturdy** stool if you cannot reach something.

Using the Microwave

- Use dishes that are microwave-safe.
- Never use **aluminum** foil or metal.
- Start with a short cook time. If you need to, add a little more.
- Use oven mitts when removing something.
- Stir liquids before and during heating.

Reduce, Reuse, Recycle!

When it comes to helping the earth, little things add up! Here are some ways to go green in the kitchen!

- Reuse plastic bags. If they aren't too dirty, you can use them again!

- Take a lunchbox. Then you won't use a paper bag.

- Store food in reusable containers instead of using plastic bags.

- Carry a reusable water bottle. Then you won't buy drinks all the time!

Measuring Tips

Wet Ingredients
Set a measuring cup on the countertop. Add the liquid until it reaches the amount you need. Check the measurement from eye level.

Dry Ingredients
Dip the measuring cup or spoon into the dry ingredient. Scoop out a little more than you need. Use the back of a dinner knife to scrape off the **excess**.

Moist Ingredients
Ingredients like brown sugar and dried fruit are a little different. They need to be packed down into the measuring cup. Keep packing until the ingredient reaches your measurement line.

Do You Know This = That?

There are different ways to measure the same amount.

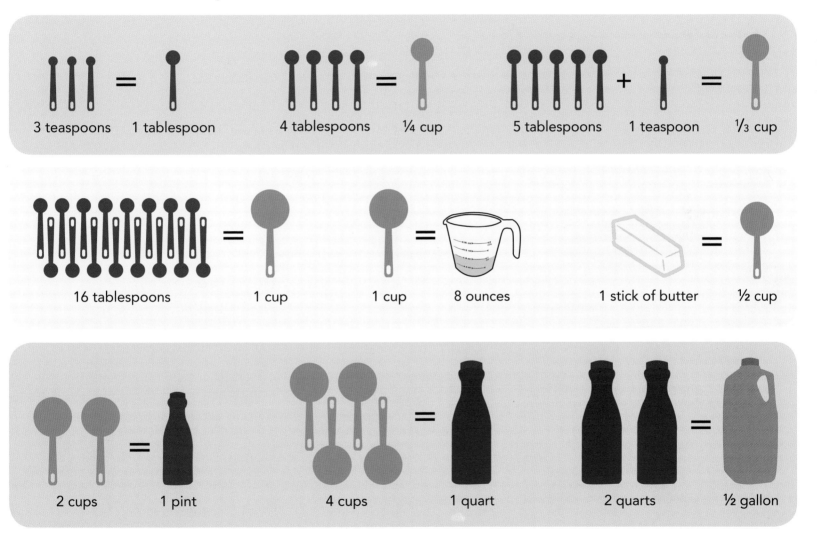

3 teaspoons = 1 tablespoon

4 tablespoons = ¼ cup

5 tablespoons + 1 teaspoon = ⅓ cup

16 tablespoons = 1 cup

1 cup = 8 ounces

1 stick of butter = ½ cup

2 cups = 1 pint

4 cups = 1 quart

2 quarts = ½ gallon

Cooking Terms

Blend

Mix ingredients together with a blender.

Chop

Cut into very small pieces with a knife.

Core

Scoop out the center using a corer.

Mash

Crush food until soft with fork or masher.

Mix

Combine ingredients with a mixing spoon.

Peel

Remove fruit or vegetable skin. Use peeler if needed.

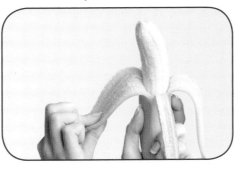

Slice

Cut into thin pieces with a knife.

Spread

Make a smooth layer with a spoon, knife, or spatula.

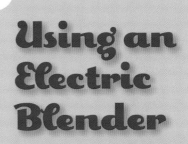

Using an Electric Blender

Put the base of blender on the countertop. Make sure the jar is locked in place. Add the liquid ingredients, then the solids. Put the lid on tight. If you don't, you'll have a big mess!

Press the pulse button until all the ingredients are mixed. Do not over blend! Before you change settings, make sure the blade comes to a stop first.

When you're finished, pour the mixture into a glass or pitcher. Wipe off the base with a wet cloth. Wash the jar and lid with warm, soapy water. Be careful with the blade!

Tools

Here are some of the tools that you'll need to get started.

aluminum foil

cereal bowl

mixing spoon

can opener

blender

microwave-safe mixing bowls

potato masher

measuring cups
(dry ingredients)

measuring cup
(wet ingredients)

measuring spoons

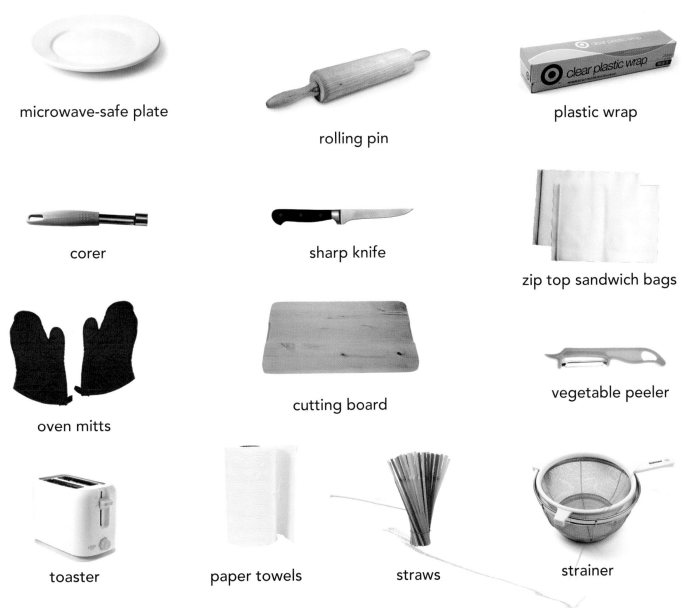

microwave-safe plate

rolling pin

plastic wrap

corer

sharp knife

zip top sandwich bags

oven mitts

cutting board

vegetable peeler

toaster

paper towels

straws

strainer

Ingredients

Fresh Produce

- ☐ apples
- ☐ bananas
- ☐ iceberg lettuce, shredded
- ☐ raspberries
- ☐ strawberries
- ☐ tomatoes

Canned Goods

- ☐ pineapple chunks
- ☐ peaches
- ☐ canned pinto beans

Baking Aisle

- ☐ brown sugar
- ☐ cinnamon
- ☐ honey
- ☐ vanilla extract
- ☐ powdered sugar
- ☐ raisins
- ☐ walnuts, chopped

Frozen

- ☐ frozen toaster waffles
- ☐ frozen raspberries in light syrup
- ☐ unsweetened strawberries

Dairy

- ☐ buttermilk
- ☐ cottage cheese
- ☐ cream cheese
- ☐ milk
- ☐ plain yogurt
- ☐ sharp cheddar cheese, shredded
- ☐ sliced cheese (any kind)

Meat

- ☐ sliced ham

Other

- ☐ crunchy granola bar (any kind)
- ☐ jam (any kind)
- ☐ lemon juice
- ☐ maraschino cherries
- ☐ oat bran
- ☐ orange juice
- ☐ peanut butter
- ☐ regular rolled oats
- ☐ bagels
- ☐ whole-wheat tortillas
- ☐ medium flour tortillas
- ☐ dried apples
- ☐ dried apricots
- ☐ dried cranberries
- ☐ waffle cone bowls

Breakfast in a Cone

A fun start to the day!

Makes 4 servings

Ingredients

2 cups cottage cheese

4 tablespoons powdered sugar

½ teaspoon vanilla extract

1 cup canned peaches, drained and chopped

4 waffle cone bowls

4 maraschino cherries

Tools

- can opener
- medium bowl
- measuring cups
- measuring spoons
- mixing spoon
- strainer
- cutting board
- sharp knife

1 In medium bowl, mix cottage cheese, powdered sugar, and vanilla until smooth.

 2 Stir in peaches.

3 Put equal amounts of cottage cheese and fruit mixture into each waffle cone bowl. Top with a cherry.

 Try canned pineapple or fresh strawberries instead of peaches.

1

2

3

Peanutty Banana Split

Dessert for breakfast!

Makes about 1 serving

Ingredients

1 ripe banana, peeled and sliced lengthwise

about 1 tablespoon peanut butter

about 1 tablespoon honey

1 crunchy granola bar (any kind)

Tools

- sharp knife
- cutting board
- plate
- measuring spoons
- dinner knife
- plastic zip top sandwich bag
- rolling pin

1 Lay sliced banana halves on plate. Spread peanut butter on top.

 2 Squeeze some honey onto peanut butter.

 3 Put granola bar in plastic zip top bag. Use rolling pin to crush granola bar to make crumbles.

 4 Sprinkle granola crumbles over top of honey. Enjoy!

17

Waffle Sandwich

Waffles to go, please!

Makes 1 serving

Ingredients

2 frozen toaster waffles

1 tablespoon
peanut butter

1 tablespoon jam
(any kind)

½ cup bananas
or strawberries, sliced

Tools

- toaster
- plate
- dinner knife
- measuring spoons
- measuring cups
- aluminum foil

1 Toast waffles according to directions on package.

 2 Spread peanut butter on one waffle with dinner knife. Top with fruit.

 3 Spread jam on the other waffle with dinner knife.

 4 Press waffles together. Eat or wrap in **aluminum** foil to go.

Try blueberry waffles in this recipe!

Rise 'n' Shine Rollup

A yummy, nutritious breakfast treat!

Makes 4 servings

Ingredients

8 ounces cream cheese, softened

2½ teaspoons brown sugar

1 teaspoon cinnamon

¼ cup walnuts, chopped

¼ cup raisins

2 apples, peeled, cored, and thinly sliced

4 whole-wheat tortillas

Tools

- measuring spoons
- measuring cups
- sharp knife
- cutting board
- mixing bowl
- mixing spoon
- microwave-safe plate
- paper towels
- vegetable peeler
- corer
- plastic wrap

1 Mix **softened** cream cheese, brown sugar, cinnamon, walnuts, and raisins in medium bowl with mixing spoon.

 2 Put tortillas between two **moist** paper towels on microwave-safe plate. Microwave on high for 15 to 30 seconds.

 3 Spread **approximately** 2 tablespoons of cream cheese mixture onto each warm tortilla. Place approximately ten apple slices on each tortilla.

4 Start at edge and roll each tortilla into tube. Wrap **leftovers** in plastic wrap and store in refrigerator up to one week.

Shake-Shake Shakes

Scrumptious smoothies!

Each recipe makes 2 servings

Ingredients

20 ounces pineapple chunks in unsweetened juice, canned and chilled

1 ripe banana, peeled and sliced

1½ cups skim milk

¼ teaspoon vanilla extract

Tools

- can opener
- strainer
- measuring cups
- blender
- sharp knife
- cutting board
- measuring spoons
- tall glasses
- straws

1. Drain pineapple, saving ¾ cup of juice. Read blender tips on page 9. Put juice and ½ cup pineapple chunks in blender. Store **leftover** pineapple in refrigerator.

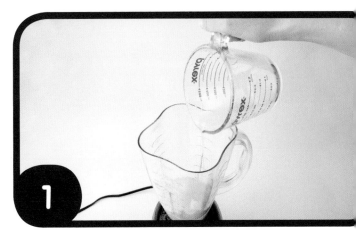

2. Put remaining ingredients in blender. Blend on medium for about 15 seconds until smooth.

3. Pour mixture into tall glasses and drink with straws.

Strawberry-Banana Surprise

½ cup frozen unsweetened (or 1 cup fresh) strawberries

1 ripe banana, peeled and sliced

½ cup orange juice

3 tablespoons plain yogurt

Raspberry-Peach Dazzle

10 ounces raspberries in light syrup, frozen

1 cup peach nectar, canned

½ cup buttermilk

1 tablespoon honey

23

Ham & Cheese Bagel

Delicious breakfast on the go!

Makes 2 servings

Ingredients

2 bagels, split in half

2 slices cheese (any kind)

2 or more slices lean ham

Tools

• sharp knife

• cutting board

• toaster

• microwave-safe plate

1 Toast four bagel halves. Place them on microwave-safe plate. Put cheese on two of the halves. Place sliced ham on remaining two halves.

2 Microwave on high for 30 seconds or until cheese begins to melt.

3 Put halves together to make two sandwiches. Eat while warm!

 Get creative with your bagel! Try sliced tomato with cream cheese and fresh basil. Yum!

Buenos Días Burrito

South-of-the-border breakfast!

Makes 1 serving

Ingredients

1 medium flour tortilla

½ cup canned pinto beans, drained and rinsed

¼ cup sharp cheddar cheese, shredded

½ tomato, chopped

½ cup iceberg lettuce, shredded

Tools

- measuring cups
- microwave-safe plate
- can opener
- sharp knife
- cutting board

Lay tortilla on microwave-safe plate. Place pinto beans and cheese in center of tortilla. Microwave on high for 45 seconds. Top with tomatoes and lettuce.

Fold tortilla over one end of filling. Fold one long side over the top. Make sure filling is tight against the tortilla.

Wrap other long end over both folds. Fold the remaining open end. Turn the burrito over so it stays closed.

Add more vegetables like black olives and green onions. Top with your favorite salsa or sour cream.

Sunny O's

A tasty change from regular cereal!

Makes 5 servings

Ingredients

1 cup regular rolled oats

1 cup plain yogurt

1 cup low-fat milk

½ cup walnuts, chopped

⅓ cup honey

¼ cup oat bran

3 tablespoons dried apricots, chopped

3 tablespoons dried cranberries

3 tablespoons dried apples, chopped

Raspberries or other fresh berries (optional)

Tools

• large bowl

• measuring cups

• measuring spoons

• sharp knife

• cutting board

• mixing spoon

• plastic wrap

• cereal bowl

Put all ingredients except the fresh berries in large bowl. Mix well.

 Cover with plastic wrap and chill in refrigerator for at least 2 hours.

3 Spoon ¾ cup mixture into cereal bowl. Top with fresh berries if desired.

29

Awesome Applesauce

An old favorite for breakfast!

Makes 2-3 servings

Ingredients

4 large apples, peeled, cored, and thinly sliced

¼ cup water

1 tablespoon lemon juice

2 tablespoons honey

cinnamon to taste

Tools

- vegetable peeler
- corer
- sharp knife
- cutting board
- microwave-safe bowl
- measuring cups
- measuring spoons
- mixing spoon
- oven mitts
- plastic wrap
- potato masher
- serving bowls

30

1 Put sliced apples in large microwave-safe bowl. Pour water over apples.

 2 Add lemon juice and honey. Stir mixture well with mixing spoon.

 3 Cover bowl with plastic wrap. Microwave on high for 5 minutes. If apples are not mushy, put them back in the microwave for 1 minute at a time until soft.

 4 Mash apple mixture with potato masher until slightly chunky.

 5 Spoon applesauce into serving bowls and sprinkle with cinnamon. Eat warm or chilled.

 The riper your apples are, the better they will work!

Glossary

aluminum – a light metal.

approximately – about or close to.

excess – more than the amount wanted or needed.

leftover – something remaining.

moist – slightly wet.

soften – to bring to room temperature or make less firm.

sturdy – strong and well built.

utensil – a tool used to prepare or eat food.

About SUPER SANDCASTLE™

Bigger Books for Emerging Readers
Grades K–4

Created for library, classroom, and at-home use, Super SandCastle™ books support and engage young readers as they develop and build literacy skills and will increase their general knowledge about the world around them. Super SandCastle™ books are an extension of SandCastle™, the leading preK–3 imprint for emerging and beginning readers. Super SandCastle™ features a larger trim size for more reading fun.

Let Us Know
Super SandCastle™ would like to hear your stories about reading this book. What was your favorite page? Was there something hard that you needed help with? Share the ups and downs of learning to read. We want to hear from you! Send us an e-mail.

sandcastle@abdopublishing.com

Contact us for a complete list of SandCastle™, Super SandCastle™, and other nonfiction and fiction titles from ABDO Publishing Company.

www.abdopublishing.com
8000 West 78th Street, Edina, MN 55439
800-800-1312
952-831-1632 fax